Finding Tranquility During Difficult Times

AN INSPIRATIONAL GUIDE

Words of Encouragement

FINDING TRANQUILITY DURING DIFFICULT TIMES

Teria R. McGhee

iUniverse, Inc.
Bloomington

FINDING TRANQUILITY DURING DIFFICULT TIMES

I am not a professional or expert on any of the subjects within this book. The words I share within are merely my opinion; from my experience, and/or my way of analyzing and dealing with life and difficult situations.

iUniverse books may be ordered through booksellers or by contacting:

iUniverse
1663 Liberty Drive
Bloomington, IN 47403
www.iuniverse.com
1-800-Authors (1-800-288-4677)

ISBN: 978-1-4759-8146-9 (sc)
ISBN: 978-1-4759-8147-6 (ebk)

Printed in the United States of America

iUniverse rev. date: 04/02/2013

CONTENTS

Dedication

To my children Sha-Qwana, Earl, Charles and Paul; there is something in each of you that is more precious than others may see. You have all been sculptured by the finest artist; you were created in the image of the Most High. May you always be motivated and inspired to live life to your fullest potential.

To my readers, may you be motivated to find tranquility in the midst of the various seasons life may take you through. May each of you recognize the unique talents and gifts you possess and use them accordingly.

ACKNOWLEDGEMENTS

I thank God for my talents, skills and abilities that were needed to write this book. I thank my pastor for imparting so many valuable lessons in Sunday services which helped to give me direction. I've been under his teaching for quite some time and have learned so much. My pastor is awesome and his words are so inspiring. His teaching has helped me in many aspects of my life, from difficult situations to college research papers and overall helping me to develop my character. He is such a wise man, when I speak, or write much of it has been inspired by his teaching. Being around positive people and a positive environment is also instrumental in helping us through the storms that life brings.

I would also like to thank my multi-talented sister Mary for helping me with the typing and editing of this book. I greatly appreciate my daughter, Sha-Qwana for her listening ear, and the most astounding advice and wisdom a mom can get from her child. To my son Earl, thank you so much for your wonderful gift, "Dragon Naturally Speaking". It came at a time when I really needed it. It has helped me a great deal by giving me the opportunity to work independently. I thank my friends, Deborah, Dorinda, Janice, Audrey and Lue for sharing their opinions on some of the subjects within this book; and most of all for being true and dependable sister friends.

PROLOGUE

In today's fast moving society we are often faced with difficult decisions, as well as situations we are unaccustomed to, or not prepared to deal with. Sometimes it's hard to find peace of mind or a peaceful solution to every situation, thus making it even more difficult to cope when under stress.

Life is full of obstacles, curve balls and challenges. Each day, every hour, every minute someone somewhere around the world will have to cope with emotional and psychological incidents: death, domestic violence, drugs, trouble in the work place or school even unhealthy or failed relationships, etc. These incidents can cause one to experience a state of depression, anger, rage, physical or mental stress. During trying times it is sometimes difficult for people to cope; situations can become so overwhelming that one loses hope.

There are many times we wonder why certain things happen to us or where our strength or faith is during these difficult times. Life with its many blows of hurt and hardships can and does take a toll on us. Often when life's challenges overwhelm us our emotions take charge. Sometimes our emotions give us strength, but there are times when our emotions let us down. It's a difficult task trying to think rationally when everything seems to be spinning out of control. As much as we would like to control situations that occur in our lives, the majority of time we feel helpless. The way we look at things makes a huge difference. How you respond to problems whether at home, work, school or even health issues depends on your perspective.

I personally have experienced and endured many trials, hardships, and unpleasant experiences. Many times I wanted to give up, but I wasn't made from that type of material. I'll stretch and bend, even give a little but, I don't wear out that easily. I have a strong resistance, especially when I know someone or something is trying to pull me down. Just knowing that someone wants to see me break, gives me the strength to fight back and I know that's the God in me. And when I come back, I come back with my full armor on, ready to fight a good fight. Now I know you don't think I mean a physical fight do you? Although I may be capable of winning one, that's not what I'm talking about. I'm talking about being prepared mentally, physically, emotionally and most of all having the correct information and knowledge to go to battle. The most intelligent, intellectual person with all types of degrees can buckle under stress. Every situation we are up against may require a different approach. Depending on the situation and circumstance you are dealing with, it may require you to do some research or soul searching. Ask questions. Question yourself—what is it that I want, what is it I need, do I have the ability to handle the situation alone, or do I need to seek assistance. What am I looking for relative to a solution to this situation? How can I overcome this addiction? How can I fight what looks to be a losing battle? How can I pull myself out of this depression? What should my next move be?

It's ok to talk to yourself and mull over things that have taken place, and your reactions to them. This only confirms that you are aware of what happened; the next step is finding the best way to proceed. You may not get the answer right away on how to proceed, but that's ok because it's not good to rush into things. Take your time and think about it; dissect what happened and brain storm different possibilities and actions you can take to approach the situation that may result in a better outcome.

There is not always a solution readily available, or a trusting person we can always talk to when these things transpire. Sometimes we are not ready to share our life events with others, but having an outlet can relieve some of the pressure. This inspirational guide was written to provide solace and tranquility during difficult times; I hope it will bring comfort to your soul and healing to your heart. It is filled with words intended to give hope, motivation, insight, and to keep you optimistic with a positive mindset during chaotic times.

Chapter 1

LEARN TO LOVE THYSELF

"Dedicate yourself to Love. Decide to let Love be your intention, your purpose, and your point. And then let Love inspire you, support you and guide you in every other dedication you make thereafter."

—Robert Holden

When I think about the word "Love" I think about 1 Corinthians 13: 4-7 which states, "Love is patient, love is kind. It does not envy, it does not boast, it is not proud. [5] It does not dishonor others, it is not self-seeking, it is not easily angered, it keeps no record of wrongs. [6] Love does not delight in evil but rejoices with the truth. [7] It always protects, always trusts, always hopes, always perseveres". (Holy Bible—NIV)

I'm sure everyone wants the love mentioned above; we want others to be patient and kind to us. We don't want to be envied, and we definitely shouldn't envy others. If we listen and take heed to this definition of love and practice being patient and kind—not dwelling on all the times we have been wronged, but loving ourselves and treating others the way we would want to be treated it would be a great start. Sometimes we have to lead by example.

I believe with love for all mankind in our heart, and casting out hatred and envy it will be easier to face and tackle difficulties which will help us deal with the emotional and physical hurt we sometimes encounter. With love comes forgiving, learning to forgive will help us understand that everyone is not perfect. When we have been wronged, we shouldn't allow it to beat us down. We shouldn't allow anger, dishonesty or bitterness to pull us down. Life will throw us many curve balls but we must learn to love ourselves. Having love for ourselves can help us more effectively deal with everything else.

By nature we should love ourselves. I believe having a great foundation to begin with can help make life a little easier, and that foundation is love.

> **"Everything has its beauty, but not everyone sees it."**
> —**Confucius**

When you love yourself you want the best for yourself. Start putting more love into what you do and the direction you want to go. Why not start by practicing giving thanks for breathing when you wake up every morning and see another day. Think positive, look at all the positive things that are going on instead of focusing so much attention on the negative. Don't waste your time building anger—thinking about those who have done you wrong, or have not been there for you. Be thankful for the family and friends that are supportive.

Surround yourself with positive motivating people. Try to stay clear of negative people or depressing situations; keep yourself in a positive and lively environment. Learn to forgive and not hold grudges. Having an unforgiving spirit can eat away at you; it can dampen your spirit and cause unwanted negative emotions. Have faith and believe that things will get better. There are so many ways we can love ourselves, there is a form of beauty in all of us, but it's often overlooked because we don't take the time to look for it.

Many times we find ourselves in compromising situations; we love others more than we love ourselves. Once we learn to love ourselves we can really appreciate love coming from someone else. We should start letting others know what we expect out of a relationship, friendship or whatever the situation may be. Instead of waiting for someone to love you, start doing things for yourself that you deserve—things that only you know how to do for you. Don't wait for someone else to do it with you or for you, take that courageous step to take care of yourself. Take time getting to know you and what works for you.

I once read somewhere, "When life gives you a hundred reasons to cry, show life you have a thousand reasons to smile."—(Unknown) We all make mistakes; a person who never made a mistake, never tried anything new. We must learn to be more optimistic; we shouldn't be too hard on ourselves.

"Embrace yourself, encourage yourself, inspire yourself, motivate yourself, educate yourself—most of all **Love Thyself".—Teria McGhee**

> *"Don't undermine your worth by comparing yourself with others. It is because we are different, that each of us is special."*
>
> *(Nancye Syms)*

Chapter 2

RELATIONSHIPS/MATTERS OF THE HEART

"Don't shut love out of your life by saying it's impossible to find. The quickest way to receive love is to give; the fastest way to lose love is to hold it too tightly, and the best way to keep love is to give it wings.

—Nancye Sims

How many times have we been in a relationship where we've felt the need to guard our hearts? Whether it's a relationship with our marriage partner, significant other, friend, or family member; when our feelings are hurt, our emotions bruised, our hearts broken, we feel emotionally sick. It hurts, whether it's intentionally done or not. Sometimes it may feel as though the world is on your shoulders. Waking up in the morning may make you wish you would have stayed asleep. Don't let life wear you down like that; stealing your joy. When your partner cheats on you and wants to walk out that door it may be time for him/her to take that walk, even more so it may be time for you to begin another journey in life. Now and then instead of trying to hold on you have to release your grip. Even when a situation doesn't look good it may work for the good. Sometimes we have to let things run its course.

Encourage yourself—pat yourself on the back, there is more to you than a broken spirit. You are a survivor, you have potential, there's a greater plan for you. You were created to do great things. This is the time for you to dig deep within yourself and challenge your potential—maximizing it and taking control of your future. As much as you may want the hurt to quickly dissipate or the situation to change for the better, change doesn't always happen right away. At times we have to go through hardships in order to appreciate the change when it occurs. Occasionally experiencing hardships helps to make us a stronger and better person. Difficulties can shape and mold our character and strengthen us. Remember you are loved, you are unique, you are beautiful; be strong, be persistent. Success sometimes requires striking out on a new path because the one you are now on is worn. Make a proclamation and demand more for yourself. Set higher standards and goals because you can and will attain them. You deserve the best and the ability to achieve greater things is within you.

In order to survive and weather the storms we have to learn to be encouraged—even encouraging ourselves, live with expectancy (expectancy of faith), believing that we can and will overcome life's obstacles, eventually finding a peaceful solution. Peace doesn't mean that we will always be trouble free—it's simply a sense of tranquility in the midst of life's storms.

> **Forgive those that hurt you so your heart will be free to love again.**
> —Nancye Sims

Failed relationships can wear heavily on a person. When someone is unfaithful, not trust-worthy, dishonest, disrespectful, or insecure it creates a strain on the relationship. It takes the effort of both partners to make a relationship work. Love, understanding, and communication are key elements to building a solid foundation in any relationship.

A relationship can lead you to a pleasant existence, or break you. When you have a good relationship with someone, cherish it. Good relationships encourage us when we are feeling down and need direction, a good relationship energizes and comforts us when we are weak and down trodden. A good relationship accepts us the way we are, and when there is something about us that needs to be addressed; it's done so in a loving way. A good relationship means that person will be there when we need them, and when we do something wrong, they will forgive us.

Developing and maintaining a healthy relationship requires time and effort. Set aside at least one day of the week for some quality time with each other, even if it's no more than an hour or two. Dine in or dine out; watch a movie or TV show together, take a walk together, read together, or play a game together.

It's been said a women's work is never done. Women often have their hands full from the time they wake up to the time they go to bed. Working a full-time job, picking up the kids from school, preparing dinner, helping kids with their homework and getting the children ready for bed makes it difficult to find quality time.

A man's schedule can be just as busy. Whether the time is spent on a business trip, hanging out with the fellows, watching or attending sport events etc. men should also examine the time they spend with their partner to see if they are giving quality time to their relationship. If you find that your are spending a significant amount of time away from your partner you may want to reevaluate the reason for this and see what can be done to include your partner in your schedule. It is important to find quality time for yourself just as you do for everyone and everything else. This will help you unwind and rejuvenate.

When trouble and problems occur in life, don't panic; this is the time when you need to take some quiet time and find ways to de-stress. I would like to share some of the things I do to keep my stress level down.

- As a Christian my first instinct is to pray. I ask God to give me the strength to deal with the situation, guiding me to a peaceful solution. If my heart is broken I ask him to help me stay strong and heal during this difficult time. I just pour my heart out to him.
- If the weather is good I go for a walk, jog, or run, whatever I'm physically capable of doing at that time. The activity helps to clear my head. I may even go to the gym or just

work out in my home. Sometimes during the physical activity I consider the situation and possible solutions, but most times I block it out and enjoy the physical activity. A physical workout usually does wonders for your mind and body, in a more relaxed state I'm able to think more clearly.

- If I have a trustworthy friend I may talk about it; sometimes talking about your problem and getting someone else's point of view, or simply getting it off your chest helps.

- If it's something I'm not ready to share with others I pray about it while giving it critical thought. I analyze the situation; put it on a scale of one to ten to see how bad the situation really is. I weigh my solution options and consider the results if handled my way. I consider the emotional results as well as what it could mean to me and the other person. I would also consider if this is a situation that requires professional counseling because sometimes we cannot always handle situations ourselves and may need professional help.

My approaches to dealing with difficulties and conflict may not work for you, but I shared them to help you to see that you do have options and that there are different approaches available and different ways you can deal with adversities.

If depression sinks in and you can't pull yourself together, look for professional help. If you don't have the finances or health coverage to seek professional help look for free services. Sometimes churches or non-profit organizations have free counseling services available.

Never be afraid to tell someone you are depressed. Depression needs to be addressed right away because it can affect you in more ways than one. According to information obtained from the Centers for Disease Control and Prevention (CDCP) "An Estimated 1 in 10 U.S. Adults Report Depression. Depression affects many Americans at different levels. Depression is a mental illness that can be costly and debilitating to sufferers. Depression can adversely affect the course and outcome of common chronic conditions, such as arthritis, asthma, cardiovascular disease, cancer, diabetes, and obesity. Depression also can result in increased work absenteeism, short-term disability, and decreased productivity."

A study found the following groups to be more likely to meet criteria for major depression:

- persons 45-64 years of age
- women
- blacks, Hispanics, non-Hispanic persons of other races or multiple races
- persons with less than a high school education
- those previously married
- individuals unable to work or unemployed
- persons without health insurance coverage

Don't let the situation get so bad that you can't function, try to get a grip on the situation as soon as you possibly can. If it becomes unbearable—too heavy of a load to carry seek help. Many times we think what we are going through is our problem alone; but that is not so. When we have family or loved ones and most of all if there are children to take into consideration, it then becomes their problem. It can affect their livelihood; they may now have to deal with the tasks which you are emotionally or physically unable to currently do. They may now have the responsibility of helping to hold together one of their loved ones. I'm sure they won't mind being there for you, but it is so important that you let a loved one know what's going on so they can give you the support you need.

Sometimes our pride or the fact that we don't want anyone to know what we are going through makes our journey more difficult. Think about it, we didn't come into this world by ourselves; our mothers helped to push us out of her womb; the doctor or midwife helped coach and monitor the birthing process. Doctors provide medicine and medical attention to keep us alive and healthy. We need the assistance of others to survive. Whether work, shelter, food, clothing, guidance, we can't do everything by ourselves; we need others to exist and live a healthy and productive life. Find someone you feel you can comfortably talk to about your dilemma; you may want to explore other resources or research and find literature that pertains to your predicament.

To get your mind off of what you are going through try pampering yourself. If finances are a problem give yourself a facial, manicure, or pedicure. Go for a walk to clear your head, do some type of physical exercise. Treat yourself to a movie, or rent a movie, (free movies and DVD's are available at your local library). Try selecting a humorous movie to pick up your spirit, or an inspirational movie to encourage and motivate you. Look for free events happening in your area. Museums and libraries offer free exhibits, seminars and workshops. Find something to do to keep your mind in a positive direction.

All things are possible when we believe; love yourself, impress yourself—work on helping your dreams come alive. Whatever you desire you can achieve if you will just believe. Turn that dream, that imagination into a plan to reach your vision, your highest potential.

> **"Today we are faced with the preeminent fact that, if civilization is to survive, we must cultivate the science of human relationships . . . the ability of all peoples, of all kinds, to live together, in the same world, at peace."**
> *—Franklin D. Roosevelt*

Chapter 3

DOMESTIC VIOLENCE

"The world is a dangerous place, not <u>only</u> because of those who do evil, but because of those who look on and do nothing."

—Albert Einstein

As domestic violence crimes have escalated there has been more support in the community and the criminal justice system. Abuse of women or men by their intimate partner is a staggering national public health problem. Facing the effects of abuse and attempting to transition, survive and maintain independence after leaving an abusive relationship can be an overwhelming experience.

It is crucial to understand that no one is immune to domestic violence. Culture, race, and ethnicity influence attitudes and beliefs about domestic violence, and these attitudes ultimately shape behavior. It is important to understand how attitudes toward domestic violence vary from culture to culture and ethnic group, to ethnic group. Victims may share the same battering event; however, their perception of the event may be interpreted differently, which may be attributed to different cultural belief systems.

There are many reasons people stay in abusive relationships: insecurity, educational, housing, financial support etc. Sometimes the victim's silence can be due to shame, isolation, embarrassment, and fear. Many times family and friends witness these acts of abuse and do nothing about it. There has to be a safe way to help, and the victim has to realize that an abusive relationship is unhealthy and unsafe. With acceptance, awareness, and education domestic violence can be suppressed. It is important that the victim know the options they have of obtaining freedom from this abuse.

Domestic violence is discussed more openly today than it was in the past. More people are getting involved to right this wrong. It is important to hear others view points, and suggestions to help these victims. There are shelters and safe houses available. Family Courts, District Attorney offices and Police Departments all have a unit just for domestic violence cases. You can go to a local hospital and let someone know if you have been abused they will give you guidance and direction. Don't worry about the financial aspect of it; once you reach out for help you will get the necessities. I've been there before I am a survivor of domestic violence so I know it's not easy to get up and leave your home, change your child's school or switch jobs so you won't be stalked or harassed. We shouldn't have to give up all these things, but sometimes it's necessary for our peace of mind and our safety, or in some cases the safety of our children.

Victims of abuse need to be empowered, they need to recognize the different alternatives they have. By willing yourself to press through the pain and discomfort you are in the process of disciplining yourself. By replacing bad thoughts and habits with positive thoughts and creating positive standards you strengthen yourself to strive for the peace of mind, and freedom from your oppressive situation. Most of all we must continue to defend the constitutional right, "the right to be free from bodily harm."

A message to all victims of domestic violence: I believe it's possible for you to rise above your limitations. It takes effort and strength to be an over-comer, but you can live a life free of abuse; it's going to take courage, faith, strength and some planning and a great bit of will power but you can do it. Don't put it off, don't wait any longer. Some people wait until a crisis arises before they begin to seek help. No smart man would ever have waited until a blizzard hit before he chopped his firewood. In the same manner, your preparation for freedom should start now, before anymore damage is done. As it states in the bible, Matthew 7: 24-25, "like a wise man who built his house on the rock. [25]The rain came down, the streams rose, and the winds blew and beat against that house; yet it did not fall, because it had its foundation on the rock; unlike the foolish man who built his house on the sand." Both encountered storms, but only those on the rock will endure." I would like to see all victims of domestic violence gain patience, endurance, maturity and confidence to break those chains that are imprisoning them. If you are not being loved and respected it's time to make a move.

> **Don't let the hurt you've experienced pierce your soul and make you cold, let it do no harm, just make you strong. Let it open your eyes and energize. All lessons learned, is knowledge gained.**
> **—Teria McGhee**

Chapter 4

PEER PRESSURE

"At any given point you can release
your greatest self. Don't let anyone
hold you back. Don't let anyone dilute
you. Don't be peer pressured into
being less than you are. People willing
to dilute themselves for the sake of
others are one of the great tragedies
of our time. Stop letting others define
and set the pace for your life. Get out
there and be your best. Do your best.
Live your best. Make every day count
and you'll see how exponentially more
exciting, thrilling, successful, happy
and full your life will be."
                                        —<u>Steve Maraboli</u>

Peer pressure is when someone tries to persuade,
or influence another to do something, or act
the way they do. Many adolescents are often
confronted with decisions and commitments that
can alter their life.

When a child advances into the adolescence stage of life he or she faces many changes and challenges. Besides having to adjust and become comfortable with the physical changes in their bodies they also encounter psychological issues along with coping academically in school. They are often faced with the pressure of picking up bad habits such as sex at an early age, alcohol, drugs and other substance abuse. Adolescents deal with peer pressure from friends, family and social life.

There are times when an adolescent can subject themselves to peer-pressure without the physical influence of another person. This can occur when an adolescent wants to fit in, or look and act the way another person does. For instance a child may notice that some of the other children's weight is less than their own; this can trigger them to go on a crash diet which can result in an extremely unhealthy weight loss. There may be a difference in body development that may influence a child to want to make changes to their own body. It could be the way the other children dresses that makes another child want to imitate or change their lifestyle to fit in, or be like someone else. Some children who develop the same habits or lifestyles tend to stick together and this can make another adolescent who doesn't have these same traits seem like an outsider, which can lead to them doing the same thing in order to fit in. This is why it is so important for a child to be taught self esteem at an early age; encouraging them that it's ok to be different and to think differently as well as to act differently.

Both male and females are faced with peer pressure but it has been said that more pressure is on the male because society and parents sometimes expect them to be able to cope and handle life events differently; this often puts a lot of pressure and stress on the male adolescent. Because males are not expected to complain, cry, and whine about certain matters this can cause them great distress which can psychologically build up and push then into a depressing state.

Peer pressure can lead to adolescent depression and adolescent suicide which has been a great area of concern lately. Depression can be for a short period of time, or it can last longer depending on the cause of the event that brought it on, and the treatment the child receives.

Trying to maintain your own identity in the face of peer pressure can be trying at times. As a young child they have their parents to guide their path and teach them certain values; this often creates a strong foundation. But once they advance into their teen years they gain independence and start branching off and making their own decisions. Some adolescents remember and adhere to the foundation their parents have set, and others want to make their own decisions. Sometimes teens put their peer opinions and values before their family; this is the starting signs of the power of peer pressure.

When children form friends they build a trust and closeness with one another. They give each other emotional support; they also see things on a different level than adults, thus creating a greater influence. If the parents have set a strong foundation and have discussed topics such as peer pressure, sex, substance abuse, gang activity and other subjects of concern with their children at a time they felt was appropriate, this could help the child when he or she is faced with dilemmas. Forming a good rapport and relationship with your child is important to their growth.

I strongly believe that your family ties and foundation have a strong influence on your self esteem. In a healthy strong bonded household where there is love, security and motivation the children often are taught values such as confidence and self worth. As parents we know that our children will make mistakes just as we did when we were growing up. Although we don't want our children to learn from mistakes, it's a part of life. We try and teach them values and fundamentals as they are growing up but we don't always cover everything. Sometimes they learn as they move along in life. Mistakes are a part of a learning process that eventually will gain you experience and wisdom.

A message for adolescents who are experiencing peer pressure: When you are confident within yourself, most likely you will learn to trust your instincts. It takes a lot of courage to be you, but it can lead to great satisfaction. Sticking to what you believe, and following your own instincts will make you more independent. Allowing yourself to be different helps you to discover who you are. It also helps you to voice your own opinion with confidence which reflects your personality. It helps build your confidence to be in control of yourself, which in turn will help you control your decisions and goals.

I believe we all have experienced some form of peer pressure, even as adults. Sometimes it may seem difficult to avoid negative peer pressure, but it is essential that you do especially when you are being persuaded to do something that can be unhealthy or harmful to you. By following the group or someone else you are allowing them to make decisions for you. Building positive self esteem can help you to resist pressure from others. Positive self esteem gives you the opportunity to feel good about yourself no matter what others may think, say, or do. It's not often, but there are instances where you find a friend that gives you positive influence. This type of peer pressure can be rewarding and possibly lead to a true friend who is looking out for your best interest by encouraging you in a positive direction.

Today there are Big Brother, Big Sister programs, mentors, and school counselors who are trained to help adolescents with peer pressure. It is important that adolescents talk with someone when they feel pressured about anything. It can be difficult for adolescents to unveil their fears or discuss their concerns with others, but having teen peer counselors or someone they are comfortable speaking with can sometimes ease that communication problem and give them the opportunity to unload the burden of the pressure they are carrying. For most young people just being able to have someone available to talk about their concerns improves their physical and mental state, and lifts their spirits.

There are programs available in high schools or outside resources designed to prevent school violence. They have teen mediators trained to listen to student concerns as well as resolve conflicts. It would be in your best interest to research and explore some of these available options.

Maturing from an adolescent into a young adult and becoming responsible is not always easy. It is important to let adolescents know the choice is theirs; they need to trust their own instincts. It is better to have positive self-esteem instead of waiting for other peoples' approval.

> **"Be proud of who you are and know that you have the ability to accomplish anything. You are unique there is no one else like you; you are special, you are beautiful, you have your own gifts, talents and abilities; let them shine and set the greatest example for yourself by being yourself."**
>
> **—Teria McGhee**

Chapter 5

SUBSTANCE ABUSE

No matter what the situation is, there is always hope. Even if you are disappointed, you can live without many things, but hope isn't one of them. So hold onto it with all your strength and remember, there's always tomorrow...

— Nancye Sims

Substance abuse has a tremendous impact on the quality of your life, education and relationships. Heavy drinking and the consumption of drugs and tobacco can contribute to an atmosphere that can be dangerous and unsafe for you and your loved ones. Excessive alcohol and drug use can cause physical deterioration, memory lapse, short attention span and difficulty concentrating. Excessive alcohol and drug use can lead to death.

You are loved—you are a beautiful specimen of mankind, you are important and your family is important and you are important to your family.

Don't let something of little or no substance ruin your life. We were created to rule over the earth and everything in it. If the earth is controlling you that means as mankind you are malfunctioning and failing to do what you were originally designed to do. Think back and remember, wasn't there a time when you were happy, carefree and drug free; wasn't it a happier time of your life? Remember yourself as a child—running, joking, laughing and playing with your friends. I'm sure you can remember some of the most happy, fun and exhilarating times of your life as you were growing up. Even as a teen before trying or knowing about any type of substance abuse I'm sure there were fun times or maybe even someone you knew who had the gift of making you laugh. They were hilarious without even knowing it, it was a natural gift they had and they used it freely. That person may have been you . . . There were so many activities and things we could do to enjoy ourselves. We didn't need alcohol or any type of drugs to get this wonderful feeling. This was a natural high from doing things we enjoyed. You can still dig up this natural high, it still exists. The only difference is it may now be clouded because you chose to use something that can cause you to act outside of the norm. What may have initially started out as a recreational way to enjoy yourself, or give you a mellow feeling has now become an addiction . . .

> Genesis 1:26 **And God said, Let us make man in our image, after our likeness: and let them have dominion over the fish of the sea, and over the fowl of the**

> **air, and over the cattle, and over all the
> earth, and over every creeping thing
> that creepeth upon the earth.**

We shouldn't allow alcohol, drugs or any other substance to control or dominate us. Everything we do should be done within reason; anything taken to the extreme becomes error. We should have power over these things—alcohol and drugs do not have the ability to operate on its own. We were not designed to let something which can't walk, talk, move or do any sort of action control us. Malfunction occurs when we allow a substance to take control of our body. It is a sign that we are relinquishing our God given powers by allowing a foreign object to manipulate and influence our reasoning power, thus rendering us helpless to reach our highest potential.

> **Every man is the temple of God and
> the dwelling place of His Spirit. But
> His Spirit will not dwell in an unkempt
> temple**
>
> **—A. R. Bernard**

Your low self esteem can chip away at everything you try to accomplish. Take charge of your life, you will never pursue your purpose if you don't think you are worth anything. Addiction can be conquered. Don't feel doomed, it's not over, you can gain control of your life again. A good start to taking control of your life can be by putting your priorities in perspective. You have the ability to make what seems impossible, possible. It may not be easy, but with a strong desire and commitment you can be on the road to recovery. You may need the help of a program, or some sort of professional counseling, there are plenty available.

A CHANGE STARTS WITH YOU

I believe we all have a survival mechanism built within us. When our back is up against the wall and all else seems lost, if we have a desire to survive, we will find the energy, will power and potential to unlock that survival kit to do battle. Change is a process. With faith, determination and a strong will power you can be as resilient as you want to be. You can conquer any fear, bondage or interruption that is taking place in your life. Once you decide to make a change in your lifestyle, it can be the start of a new beginning. All change begins with a decision and should be followed by dedication, discipline and planning. Be a happier person, it's the choices that you make that will determine your happiness.

> **Without a vision for the future you will always live in the past.**
> **—A. R. Bernard**

> **Change enriches you; it gives you New life, New courage, New strength, New hope, New dreams. So go ahead and make a change you know is for the best. You'll be happier and glad you did** . . .
> **—Nancye Sims**

Chapter 6

UNEMPLOYMENT

The by-product is that the more people you help, the "richer" you become, mentally, emotionally, spiritually, and definitely financially.
    —T. Harv Eker Quotes from Secrets of the Millionaire Mind

"Most of the important things in the world have been accomplished by people who have kept on trying when there seemed to be no hope at all."
    —Dale Carnegie

If you're unemployed don't let depression sink in, think about the positive aspect of it; maybe it's time for a change in your life. If you have bills to pay and no savings and you're not eligible for unemployment income, take the time to see what type of City, State or Government assistance is available for you; do research to see what charity or non-profit organizations may be available to assist you with food, utilities, shelter and employment referrals. Sign up for volunteer work; this will help keep you busy and at the same time may be an opportunity to learn a new skill. This very volunteer job may consider you for a permanent position.

Use your spare time to help someone else instead of worrying about what you don't' have. Offer to help the elderly in your neighborhood by going to the store for them, helping to tidy their home or just giving them some positive conversation, or a listening ear. Through giving you never know what you may receive; it could be a word about an available position, an idea of how to create some income or just the joy of being able to lift someone else's spirit will lift and bring joy to yours. Most often when we do something good for others it makes us feel good about ourselves and keeps our mind off what we are going through. Occasionally we may realize that what we thought was a difficult situation is really not that bad and we recognize we have options. Consider what others may be going through, as the saying goes, "things can always be worse". Try to find something positive in what you believe to be a difficult time.

Use this time to sharpen your skills and further your education, it's ultimately up to us to discover and uncover our destiny. No matter how much negativity tries to sneak in, look for the positive aspects of the situation and overpower it. Take time to get to know yourself and exercise the God given talents you have which may help you advance in life. I believe most successful people are using their God given talents. This may be a time for you to recognize your skills and creativity to start your own business, write a book, poetry, songs, or learn a second language or another trade. The spare time you now have due to unemployment may open the door to many new adventures that you never had the time to explore when you were working with a busy schedule. Don't look at it like it's the end of the world—look at it as a new season in your life. Yes it may call for adjustments and a change in your lifestyle, but change can be a great new positive and refreshing start to a new you.

One thing we have to keep in mind whether employed or unemployed and that is how to budget your money. If someone is unemployed they definitely don't need to spend money unnecessarily. When shopping, we should always ask ourselves the following questions:

- Do I need this item, or is it just something I want?
- If it's not a necessity and I go ahead and purchase it, will I be neglecting something else?
- Can I handle the consequences of neglecting something because of my wants?

There are ways you can come up with a few dollars to help out during this difficult time:

- Sell your items at a flea market or have a garage sale (your trash is someone else's treasure)
- Sell your items on Amazon or E-bay, do your research there are other organizations that will purchase your items.

- Maybe it's time to cash in those pennies or loose change you've been saving.
- Can you knit, crochet, sew, or cook? (Using these skills to make something someone can use could be profitable)
- You may want to consider selling Avon or look into other money earning opportunities that don't require a start up fee

Some of these suggestions may not bring in a large sum of money but it may be able to generate an amount that can help you pay a small bill, transportation fee/keep gas in your car, groceries, etc. Remember being able to pay one bill is better than not being able to pay any; and keep in mind there is always someone worse off than you, so be thankful for what you do have. Whatever you do, don't give up, you know the saying, "Winners never quit and quitters never win." Always try to brainstorm and put a plan into effect, "If you fail to plan; you plan to fail".

That's life, things happen; as the saying goes, "Change is the only thing that is constant." It's only natural when circumstances arise for us to feel disappointed, our feelings and emotions get involved and we want to shout or cry; but don't let obstacles overwhelm you—face them, embrace them, step back and take some quiet time to look at them from a different perspective. Don't worry about gossip, things you can't change, people who don't like you, things that didn't go as planned, unexpected circumstances. If we take the time to look we can find a lot of positive in something we initially see as a negative or bad situation. Be comforted knowing that you can find the knowledge and strength to get through the rough times.

> **"Don't give up when you still have something to give. Nothing is really over until the moment you stop trying."**
>
> —**Unknown**

Chapter 7

MOTIVATION

Without motivation there is no inspiration

(Teria McGhee)

Throughout life we should learn to discipline, encourage and motivate ourselves. Motivation keeps the wheels of life turning. We are spiritual beings mastering the ways of life. We can't think or believe that our success lies solely in the hands of someone else. We should learn how to motivate ourselves and believe in the gift of faith especially during the times of trouble and stress. Faith is a tiny seed that will grow larger and stronger the more you use it.

Don't beat up on yourself because you made mistakes or bad decisions, who on this earth hasn't? You are entitled to be forgiven and deserve the chance to get up, dust yourself off and try it again. If you can't do it by yourself, if it hasn't worked thus far, put that pride to the side and ask for help. Time is precious; don't waste it. Accept help, take a hold of that lifeline, pull yourself up, and get ready to start the good life.

Forgive and let go of the anger and hurt caused by those who have abused you, used you, lied on you, ridiculed you or stole from you. We are so much more than a puppet on a string. Take charge of your own life; bring that puppet to life and live your life the way you were destined to. Cut those strings that are being controlled by something or someone. Breathe life back into that lifeless body—that tired soul. It's time to stop letting drugs, alcohol and people control you. It's time to walk away from that life of abuse because anyone who abuses you doesn't love you. You were born to enjoy the fruits of this life. Yes there will be hard times but if we all learn to be supportive to one another these situations will be more endurable. Don't kick someone when they are down, this is the time they need you the most. "When you're kind to others, you help yourself; when you're cruel to others, you hurt yourself." "The one who blesses others is abundantly blessed; those who help others are helped." (Message Bible, Proverbs 11:17)

From the young to the elderly, why not reach out and help those who can't help themselves. Is it asking too much to lend a helping hand, a listening ear, a smile, a kind word, food for the hungry, or clothing? You may know someone who has no income, or just lost their job; they may be in need of food, toiletries, a metro card or items for their children. We should practice lifting each other up with polite words and being more supportive during someone's time of need. When someone is going through hard times do not add to their burden by being unkind and difficult; this is the time to show brotherly love and give whatever support you can. If you are able to assist, offer a helping hand, don't gossip or speak ill about their misfortune.

Don't give up on life; live life—it's free! Life is meant to be lived to the fullest. You have the capability to reach far and enjoy everything within this universe. Live wisely, we all will experience pain and shame and many times the road may seem rough and the journey long, but through our trials and tribulations we gain knowledge. As the saying goes, "Life is not a destination but a journey"; live and learn, don't squander your precious life. Gain wisdom for it is better than wealth. The hardest thing to do is what is right, when you make that decision to do right you set yourself free, you release the bondage.

We must recondition ourselves, our way of thinking, and the way we react and respond in order for us to be able to deal with adversities. Often we think we are not capable of being successful or accomplishing certain things. This attitude stems from many suppressive forces that direct our thinking toward mediocre levels. I believe this is why we need to communicate and spend time in the presence of motivating people who are concerned and knowledgeable about the situations we are dealing with. According to another quote I received during Sunday service, "We become servant to the choices we make; our life is composed of our choices, and our choices determine our destiny."

When faced with difficult situations it can become overwhelming trying to figure out how to tackle them. We have to remember that we are not alone and there are resources available. Attending empowerment groups, seeking counseling, reading motivational material; or speaking to your pastor can bring inspiration and give you a sense of direction.

I am a domestic violence survivor; I was once in a very depressing state. I felt caged—as if I didn't have anywhere to turn; but once I reached out and accepted help, things changed. The inspirational and motivational assistance I received through counseling and other governmental agencies along with prayer and support from family and friends helped me emerge from the imprisoned—like state I felt trapped in. I became skilled at opening up and communicating with others more easily. I learned to move from quantity to quality. It didn't matter anymore if I had to pay all the bills by myself, because my children and I now felt safe, and we had peace of mind. It didn't matter if I couldn't go shopping for clothes or have extra spending money, because I realized once I had my necessities I was blessed. All of this happened because my values had shifted and I was looking at things from a different perspective. I then realized the true value of the things that had been removed, the ones I didn't want to let go of (In actuality they weren't valuable at all). Sometimes we are so comfortable in our environment because we have been there so long that we don't realize the atmosphere we are living in has become toxic and it is in our best interest to move on. I then started to build my life by revelation knowledge, not by feelings and circumstances. So my point is that, we sometimes have to learn to change our perspective, when we can't immediately change our problems.

I also believe motivation plays a key role in using our communication skills while operating under stress. I believe sometimes people need an intercessor to help pave the way. It is a true statement that attitude determines approach, and approach determines success or failure. Many times when dealing with troubled or depressed individuals we discover that they don't know the extent of their oppressed situation, or how to overcome it; they need help coming out of the cage. Having someone with motivating skills around can help you build the confidence and communication power you need to move forward. As motivational speaker Les Brown states, "It's not over until you win." Brown speaks with strength, confidence and a sense of assurance that makes you feel you can overcome anything. Brown teaches people to be a "Victor" and not a "Victim." I believe it is possible to rise above our limitations. It takes effort and strength to overcome, but with motivation as a source of help we can gain the patience, endurance, maturity, and confidence to find peace in any situation. Sometimes problems serve a purpose in our lives, they help us develop skills in finding solutions to difficult situations.

Communication is so important; it is one of the most powerful tools we possess. Talking is the conduit through which information travels; learning the art of communicating well and utilizing the right sources could possibly make any situation less difficult to deal with. Words have creative power and can carry emotions that create joy, sadness, or doubt, but once you know who you are and recognize your talents and abilities you won't let those qualities be stripped from you; you learn to brush off those hateful words that people use to try to hurt your feelings and destroy your character.

Besides using the communication tools we should keep in mind, that with problems come solutions. We must concentrate on keeping ourselves calm because tension builds a blockage which interferes with our rational thinking power. Under stress your brain doesn't operate efficiently. With a relaxed mind the solution will come forth with clarity. Assemble the facts sensibly, without partiality and relative to your situation. Once that has been established you will be able to see things more clearly and objectively.

Our mind is an incredible device. Your state of mind can propel you to great success or major destruction, depending on your thinking process. Just as food is fuel for your body, the mind operates on what it is being fed. Communicating with the right sources can help you learn how to handle difficult situations that make you feel cornered. Spending excessive time with people that have petty and negative attitudes will have you thinking petty and negative. On the other hand, close contact with individuals that have big ideas and ambitions will raise your level of ambition. Be careful, observe the environment you're in and the one you create; practice creating positive energy to ward off the negative forces.

Many times we are quick to put the blame on someone else for our circumstances. I've learned that the first step in developing self-control is to accept responsibility for your lack of self control and to admit what your problem is. From time to time you have to talk back to your feelings and challenge some of those subconscious attitudes; practice mastering your thoughts and moods.

Too many times those who have been hurt and don't want to face reality bury their emotions. When we have problems that we need to talk about; we should look for someone who will keep our problems confidential and not choose someone who is known to talk too much. We should avoid situations that weaken our self control and those that will cause temptations in our lives. There is a saying I recall, "There are two primary things that waste our time: regret and worry. "When we regret the past, we waste time looking backward to change something we can't change anyway."

If you are reading this, you have survived your entire life up until this very moment. You have survived many trials and tribulations, pain, suffering, heartbreak and many other chaotic seasons of life. You obviously are stronger than you think you are. You are awesome ... continue to push forward, believe and take notice of the many great expectations in store for you.

> **Don't be afraid to admit you are less than perfect. It is this fragile thread that binds us together.**
> **—Nancye Sims**

EPILOGUE

I hope this book has allowed you to see how viewing things in a different perspective can lead to positive results. Learning to view life events in a different perspective will show and prove everything is not as bad as it initially seems.

- ❖ Closed doors can now lead to opportunities for another door to open
- ❖ Losing an old friend can lead to new true friends
- ❖ Leaving a toxic relationship can lead to freedom, peace and a stress free life
- ❖ Losing a job can open doors to a new career, the start of your own business, it can help you recognize your creativity and maximize your God given talents.
- ❖ It can allow you to recognize the courage and strength you have hidden inside
- ❖ Respect and Love yourself, people will treat you the way you allow them to
- ❖ Never underestimate yourself by saying, "I can't do it", if something has been done before it can be done again.
- ❖ The list can go on and on; life is what you make it . . .

If you have been inspired by this book take the time to inspire someone else; whether it's with a kind word, a compliment or a helping hand; just as one hand washes the other . . .

A Message from the Author

I hope you enjoyed the topics within this book; if you were pleased with the inspiring words please be on the look-out for my next book of motivational and inspirational topics. If you have a specific topic you would like to see in my upcoming books you may email your suggestions to: WordsofInspirations@ gmail.com

REFERENCE

"An Estimated 1 in 10 U.S. Adults Report Depression." Center for Disease Control Prevention, Web. 10 Dec. 2012. <http://www.cdc.gov/features/dsdepression/>.

Bernard, A.R. *Happiness Is* . . . . 1st ed. New York: Simon & Schuster, Inc., 2007. 125. Print.

Bernard, A.R. *Happiness Is* . . . . 1st ed. New York: Simon & Schuster, Inc., 2007. 151. Print.

Brown, Les. *It's Not Over Until You Win*. Print.

Holy Bible, New International Version®, NIV® Copyright © 1973, 1978, 1984, 2011 by Biblica, Inc.® Used by permission. All rights reserved worldwide.

Peterson, Eugene H. *The Message (MSG)*. 1993, 1994, 1995, 1996, 2000, 2001, 2002 . Web. <http://www.biblegateway.com/passage/?search=Proverbs 11&version=MSG>.

Sims, Nancye. "Writings of Nancye Sims." *nancyesims.com*. N.p., n.d. Web. 10 Dec 2012. <http://nancyesims.com/>.

About the Author

Teria R. McGhee is a Native New Yorker, born in the borough of Brooklyn, New York. She is a mother of four, and a grandmother of two. Teria has a Bachelors Degree in Psychology and a Masters Degree in Urban Studies and Certification in Public Administration. Teria has finally completed one of her goals by putting her thoughts on paper. Her desire in creating this book is that it will be instrumental in helping others as they go through various storms life takes us through.

Printed in the United States
By Bookmasters